Lunessence

A Devotional for Selene

Edited by Callum Hurley

BIBLIOTHECA ALEXANDRINA

Selene by K.S. Roy

For the Silver Lady
That by this votive you shall know
That ever the hearts of men
Will wash upon your dusty shores

Selene Medallion

Table of Contents

Introduction

I sit here now, in my editorial duties, thinking of just what words I can justly give of Selene.

She is not simply a Goddess who moves with words, but the glorious silver light that men have gazed at in wonder since time immemorial. She is the indefinable spirit of the night, gentler than the hot and boisterous day. She is peace and rest. My attempt here to put into so few words everything that she is and means to us would be as wrong as it would be futile.

So I shall dare to say only this:

Love of the Moon has been common to every culture and time, and to the Ancient Greeks this took the form of Selene. Indeed, I have loved the Moon for as long as I can recall; our relationship stretches back into the mists of my very own personal prehistory in just such the same manner. My aim in putting together this work was to share in that same feeling from the perspective of others both ancient and modern, united in essence across the vastness of time. And in this I have certainly not been disappointed.

Selene was regarded as something of a universal/celestial figure by the Greeks, unconstrained to a single location or form, but present everywhere and for all. I was delighted to find that same spirit alive and well within this anthology — there really is a little bit of everything here. I am moved deeply by the efforts of all of the wonderful people whom this book has singularly united in their celebration of this myth. I cannot offer thanks enough for their efforts and for sharing their love of the Moon with my own.

Allow me to express my gratitude to all, contributor and reader alike, for granting me the opportunity to be a part of this process. If you enjoy the book even a fraction as much as I enjoyed overseeing its creation, then I will consider my labors to have been worthwhile.

So please enjoy, and O épainos eínai sto Selene!

Callum Hurley
Autumn 2015

From the Desk of the Editor-in-Chief

by Rebecca Buchanan

My path to Hellenismos was a rather round-about one. As a little girl, I adored Greek mythology, particularly stories about Goddesses. Artemis, Athena, Aphrodite, Hekate — yep. When I eventually discovered Selene (and Her sister Eos and her brother Helios), I was seriously disappointed by the dearth of stories about them.

The best-known is that of Endymion, the shepherd whom Selene loved and who was granted eternal youthful sleep; by him, She became the mother of fifty daughters and (possibly) one son. She is also said to have borne three daughters to Zeus; to have been involved somehow in the creation of the Nemean Lion which later fought Herakles; and to have been pursued romantically by the pastoral God Pan.

Additionally, she is mentioned frequently in the works of ancient playwrights and poets and philosophers, such as Aeschylus, Euripides, Plato, Sappho, Corrina, Homer, Apollonius Rhodius, Quintas of Smyrna, Ovid, and Virgil, to name a few — but she is rarely the focus of these writings. She is in the background, up above, shining Her light on another's grand adventure. Selene (and Eos and Helios) was a secondary character in the larger cosmology.

This struck me as strange: surely the Moon and the Dawn and the Sun were just as important, just as worthy of stories, as the Goddesses of Wilderness and Wisdom and Love and Magic.

I never outgrew my love of mythology, but it was not until many years later that I discovered other people who not only shared that love, but who actively honored the Old Gods and Goddesses. Even better, many of them were just as fascinated by and devoted to the "lesser-known" Deities as me.

And so we find ourselves here. I am honored to present you with *Lunessence*, the first (to my knowledge) modern devotional anthology in honor of Selene, the Lady of the Moon, the Mother of the Stars, the sister of Sun and Dawn. I hope that the poems, prayers, rites, stories, artwork, and essays within will inspire you to honor this most ancient and beautiful of Goddesses, as well — and, perhaps, write a few poems and rituals of your own.

Rebecca Buchanan
Autumn 2015

P.S. Yes, there will someday be a devotional anthology for Eos, as well, and hopefully Helios, too.

Poems and Prayers

Lunessence by Callum Hurley

Her Silver Tears

by Madaline Stevens

Her silver tears fall upon the grass
The dew drops glitter under her gaze
The pond is now a mirror, turned to glass
Under her soft dreamlike rays

A woman gently enters the moonlit grove
Dressed in only a flowing white gown
As she opens her heart to this heavenly trove
The Queen of Stars yearns to be drawn down

She dances the circle, letting her passions free
As she breathes in the scent of mystery and night
The waves of power rise, they become the sea
Their shared joy of life burns as the sun is bright

She is one, two, together, the same
We all share Selene's eternal flame

Gravity

by Luque Spinner

You stare us in the eye at night
Barefaced and unashamed
Brilliant, smiling; so, so bright,
Even when you're waned.

As we sleep we feel you go
Riding through the sky,
Your horses, whinnying in your glow,
Taking you low to high.

We ebb and flow with your direction
From birth, to death, and through,
But deny much your introspection
Though when we pay you've no issue.

You help us back to try again,
Forgiving our mistakes,
Trying to help us contend,
Trying to sooth our aches.

We love you or we curse you raw,
But even when we scoff your name
We stare at you in awe
And you stare back unashamed.

Hymn to Selene 1

by Rebecca Buchanan

I sing of
Mene, the
curly-horn'd, the
night-veil'd Queen of
Stars, who travels the arc of
heaven on the back of her
divine bull, lightning-sired, lady
of laughter and joy sweet as the dew

Hymn to Selene II

by Rebecca Buchanan

bright curling ram's horns:
hair of deepest night:
gown of moonlight and shadow:
in the stillness
before the dawn
you embrace your lover
in his bed of sweet grass and soft flowers:
fifty daughters you have borne
womb swelling
and a lone sleepless son:
does he feel your kisses?

10,000 Realms

by Callum Hurley

Through 10,000 realms may be
bound our miens with silver thread
May we live together, suffer together
Be forever born together
And finally leave this world together

*Author's note: The number 10,000 is often used in Buddhist literature as a figurative metaphor for uncountable vastness, i.e. the '10,000 realms' indicates the boundlessness of existence across an infinite number of lives. This piece was inspired by a popular ancient Chinese wedding vow, which translates roughly as "May we always be born together". It expresses a desire that, no matter where karma and the Universe might take the eternal selves or under what circumstance, that they will never be separated and that one will not accept enlightenment and bliss without the other.

(The new moon does not shine)

by James B. Nicola

The new moon does not shine, but can possess
you differently, with the absence of light.
If you are tired, for instance, and the night
is overcast so you can barely see
anything — for this you would have to be
in the country, with no street lights, unless
you found a dark spot in a town — I know
a few around here and would not mind show-

ing you, if you happened to be inclined. ...
Well, anyway, if you manage to find
a place to lie down, on a stretch of grass —
raw grass is better than a blanket, though —
you start to feel as moist as the night, and —
this is something you might not understand
until you do it, that is, manage to pass
a no-moon night out in the night — you might

dissolve, or seem to, as if you became
the air, the dark, the wet, the grass, the land.

A full moon rules. But when the moon is new
(or when the sky is overcast) the whole
night does, as if it were swallowing you
or being swallowed by you, or your soul,
which is, on such nights, just about the same.

Another Moon and Sky Poem

by James B. Nicola

If you want to see the moon
    whisper
you must look. Closely. Not just
    listen.
Do you see her hover, floating,
    silent?
Watch her rise or invisibly
    lower.
There. You see the bough? (Don't be
    standing
in the open if you'd see her
    murmur;
Stand, not right beneath, but near
    a tree.)
See the fingered branch half-veil
    her face
and see the leaf-nails ripple with
    her breath
behind — beyond — the veil? Speak! She'll
    answer
with either sudden stillness or
    another
susurrous swell of delicious
    mystery.
What she says, what she means
    may be
a different matter. But you know she
    summons

oceans and lakes into clouds
　　and mists
and fogs and wisps so that even in
　　daytime
she can don a veil at will
　　up there
queen of the night, duchess of
　　the day
in her dark or light, wonderful,
　　thunderful
overful, underful sky.

The Girl in the Moonlight

by Gerri Leen

The girl in the moonlight
dances so freely
twirling the sun's way
shaping the pattern
back to the altar
building her power
calling the forces
wielding her magic
wherever she touches
flowers spring forth.

The queen in the moonlight
regally standing
arms out before her
singing the secrets
out to the altar
starting the passions
setting her fires
joyful fruition
wherever she glances
abundance is found.

The crone in the moonlight
silently stooping
calls to all creatures
none can resist her
come to the altar
taking within her

all that is living
healing, transforming
where once she stood
now is a girl

Selene

by Gerri Leen

The moon's light shines
through the crack in my curtains,
falling on my face.
I awaken.
I feel Her power,
calling me back:
Get up. Get up.
Come dance with me;
the night is warm
The priestess blood within me
runs slow.
Another time, another night.
I turn away,
block out her light.
But in my dreams,
I dance.

Selene

by Matthew Wilson

Selene, shine down your beauty from tranquil seas
illuming woodland glades where secret lovers lay
Where you first set eyes upon Endymion sleeping
Then spirited him away before the coming of day.
Sweep the stars into position from your silver steed
Those silent watchers burning jealous at your
      beauty
So even mighty Zeus from the mountain may notice
Making drunk bets with Pan to take you from your
      duty.

Give a world your fifty daughters to claim the ages
Poets admiring wonders their sleeping father missed
Writing of Pompeii's fate or Artemis' temple
      burning
Stealing through moonlit glades where secret lovers
      kissed.

Conversion

by James B. Nicola

Travel, the purchase of perspective
on people as of place, can perch
a person at a new prospect
to heaven.

One clear and lasting night,
one summer at 8700 feet
invigorated by community
and primed, having slept under meteor showers
en plein air for the first time the previous week,
I glanced west to the lowering, glowering face of
        the moon —

Pock-marked, her cheeks; her brow, furrowed
from wisdom if not terrain,
the conscientious moon looked down, vain,
and would be noticed.

She always has, I recollect, but,
town and city-bred,
used to glance only passingly,
so varied was the glitter-grime I'd known.

But that night in the mountains, she dipped
then rose then dipped again in a nod,
a silent senior ever in the room,
about to speak her peace.

It could have been the trick of those dark hills
passing in the foreground;
or ghastly light refracted from the horizon
swelling her to a giant, dipping her twice;
or misdirection of her rhinestoned cowl. …

But smitten as if by a wink, I stopped,
gazed on her mien, no longer elderly,
and though I know she had no lips to move,
I heard.

Appeal to Selene

by Callum Hurley

I have lived amongst beasts
I have lived amongst Men
Now I long to live amongst the stars
With you

What bribe must I give the ferryman?
What words must I offer Hermes?
To embark upon those Silver shores
At last

Refuge in Beauty

by Callum Hurley

If you need me
You can find me amongst the stars tonight
In the eye of the Moon
At Selene's side, by her hand
In her land, her attendant

I'm leaving behind this Earth
Just for tonight
A refuge in beauty

In Pearl'd Mask

by Kyria Skotas

    the dreamers know Her
   slumbering through the echoed night.
                        Her pale light pooling,
at their fingers,
       the dreamers wake to dewy
                            might.
     Her gifts, on their sleep-worn
             faces,
                  as kisses stolen in the light.
Oh
      ever changing, glowing Goddess
    stretch your light to stir
             my own!
And in my dreaming, inspiration,
       Let my fingers
             know your song.

On the road when the Moon almost is full
by Barbara Ruth

Early Old Moon

by Karen Greenbaum-Maya

Got up early this morning
  to see the old moon.
Late-year's late sunrise
  gives more time
to see that last paring
  just barely turn away,
catching the last
  of this round's light.
Luminous clear cobalt sky
  will smudge like tarnished brass.
Soon the opposite sliver
  will show up between sun and night,
reversed, obscured by smog,
  dulled to dried blood.
I crave the moon after its travels,
  purified of past days.
Look, there it floats, fainter, fading.
Find it if you can before light
      puts it out.

*(Previously published in **Untamed Ink**, 2008)*

Sourdough Moon, Esalen

by Karen Greenbaum-Maya

Fire pit next to our cabin held gray,
the cooling charcoal of the ritual fire
laid for the cook. She died
in the dark of the moon,
the day before the workshop began,

her last act emptying a bowl
of moon-gold sourdough starter
rousing flour paste into foamy sponge,
giving tenderness to dough
stiff with rye and oats.

First night at dinner, I slowed down, chewed
rye berries' lean sweetness
in her last dark slack bread.

Selenic Haiku

by Callum Hurley

Beyond this vague world
The silver lady gazes
Eye as sharp as light

*Selene Aiglie ('Selene Radiant') – Ancient Greek
lettering in Shodo style Calligraphy Scroll*
by Callum Hurley

Ode to Selene

by Callum Hurley

Resplendent maid, O'Titaness benign
I sing this song of thee on cricket's stave
A softly hymn to wist the whole night through
An' at the dawn be nourished with thine dew

Upon your form, star-speckled diadem
Pir'cing the night without leaving a trace

Selene

by Vonnie Winslow Crist

Pale goddess, you gave
your name to science: selenology,
but we've relegated you to myth —
and so you continue to drift
an inch further from earth each twelvemonth.

Seventeen thousand years ago,
you would have appeared larger, more regal —
surely the inspiration
for a Paleolithic figure discovered
in southwest France who clasps
a bison horn in her right hand, raises
its notched crescent heavenward,
and touches her abdomen
with her left palm.

There are thirteen notches
slashed in the horn, equal to
the thirteen lunations per annum,
the thirteen menstrual cycles per year.

Perhaps it was a man
who shaped this primitive statue,
but I like to think it was a woman
who recognized
the salty tides of ocean and womb
are connected to the moon
and every twenty-nine-and-a-half days

celebrated
her link with Selene.

*(Previously published in **River of Stars** by Vonnie Winslow Crist)*

<u>Full Pulse</u>

by Barbara Ruth

Full moon, eclipsed
copper moon. They said
you would be blood red
but I say copper
the taste of blood
moon in my mouth
full moon
swallowing/swallowed
my sadness eclipsed but swollen, still.

First night of Pesach
no seder to go to
anxiety/
depression
depression/
anxiety
trudge through my days
boring me, shaming me
but now
the night
and the full eclipsed moon
and I run
from inside
to outside
watching you moon
and writing you moon
and making in you

my Cancer hearth.

Some have the seder and the moon tonight
and some have neither.
Some are locked up and never see the moon.
Some are invited and refuse the seder.

I make my seder in the moon
roundness of the egg, the orange, the potato,
the ritual objects we add to the seder plate.
The plate itself, the moon is my seder plate
I tilt to find
the wink of wholeness
the pulse of half
crescent
pulse
whole
pulse
my life
in that seder plate of a moon.
All I miss by not living a more Jewish life.
All I miss by not tending my flame among the Fire
          Keepers
not learning to read the Potowatomi wampum belt
as well as our diaspora.
All I miss by not going deep into the barefoot night
and looking up.

Hadn't I planned to live on lesbian land
where we celebrate the first night of seder
with our collectively written Haggadah
and our charosets from Argentina, Morocco and
          Yemen?
Hadn't I planned to grow old with dykes
who would howl the moon round
and drum the eclipse
and raise our signing hands
and ululate
and pulse?

Red moon, I see you embrace your penumbrial self
weeping for all you have not done.
Your tears reach the seas and you wonder
"Am I causing the oceans to rise?
Am I wiping out islands,
making high tide refugees
when all I ever wanted was to offer
refuge?
What is this blood staining me?
Is it the menses of women who swell to my call?
Is it the blood of war?"

My friend is two days past her due date.
The red cord that bound me to her at the Blessing
          Way
hangs from my wrist.
I wait for her word to know when to cut it

and release her daughter into the world.
Surely the copper moon will bring the birth.

Surely I too
will be pulsed in, pushed out
into the wild red world.

*[First appeared in **Snapdragon: A Journal of
Healing**. Reprinted here with kind permission.]*

Hymn to Endymion

by Rebecca Buchanan

in his cave
Endymion lay
upon his bed of purest
ram's wool, in his cave
Endymion does dream of
daughters fifty, their
smiles lost to him as he
sleeps, Endymion,
in his cave

Moonbeam

by Melia Brokaw

A crossroad on a full moon night.
I move toward it in bare feet,
bathing in the silvered white light
of the beautiful glowing orb.
Growing large in my sight
a pale feminine face smiles down
wreathed in pale light and wavy hair.
I hear the clearing of a feminine throat
and see a tendril flow downwards
like living mist or a floating ribbon,
a moonbeam moving with intent
heading straight towards me.
I blink in surprise and the beam is gone,
only to find myself astride the light.
I feel her smile, her delight, her amusement
as I'm taken for a ride through the night.
Our movement sweeps my hair back
causing a sigh of contentment, of peace;
fears, doubts and worries wash away
Curiosity causes me to study my ride
yet the harder I look the less I can see
a form of light, maybe some scales;
solid wherever it touches my own form
yet with no definition only iridescence.
A feeling of minor indecision,
a chuckle, a shrug, just the joy of the ride

as through the night we glide
content in each other's company.

Passed On

by Barbara Ruth

The last Saturday in October
Fall festival at the Springs
outdoors in the balmy air,
a bounce house
a cake walk
ping pong paddles and a table
chickens, colts and lambs.
children dressed in Halloween costumes
oldies from a boombox.

Evie smiled at the children,
tapped her foot to the tunes,
turned her face to Autumn Arizona sun
so softly warm
so good to go outside this time of year.
She said hello to neighbors, staff and kids.
Lunch was served outdoors but she only wanted
         Sprite.
And then she said, "Can we go back now?"

Back in her apartment
She took off her glasses, took out her hearing aids,
lay down on her new bed. And
then she said, "My tummy hurts."
Ane brought her Pepto Bismo and then
she said, "Did Bob call?"
Ane reminded her he usually comes on Sunday,

he'd been there last on Wednesday afternoon.

Ane asked her how she felt and then she
said, "I'll be fine."
She dozed a little, woke,
and then she said
"Ane, I'm going to die."

She didn't say, "Call the doctor, call my
children, dial 911." She didn't argue when Ane said
it wasn't true.

That afternoon I walked among the trees, so dark
            and deep
felt the crunch of changing maple leaves,
just for a second I thought of her,
teaching me to love the lovely woods,
teaching me to keep my promises.

She took a nap late that afternoon.
didn't go to the dining room for dinner.
Life had filled her up
as she filled the hearts of her parents, sister,
husband, children, students,
and all who called her friend.
Her promises had been fulfilled,
no more miles to go.

Sun in Scorpio, the day before the full moon,
a week before Dia de los Muertos,
Evelyn Marjorie Sturtz Kell joined her ancestors

— my ancestors.

This is the way I want to go
last hands that touch my body
last voice I hear
someone I love
somebody who loves me.
My last day on planet earth
I want to go outdoors
animals and children all around me
music that I love
knowing I'm a part of all of it
knowing it's my time, my journey is complete.

Okay Mom, you had the perfect death.
Now come back and tell us all about it.
And if you can't do that, could you please send a
        forwarding address,
record your new number on your answering
        machine?

When I was small we used to sing together
driving through the night:
"I see the moon, the moon sees me
The moon sees the one I long to see."

I don't know where to find you, Mom,
So I'll look for you in the moon.
I don't know the area code for where it is you've
        gone,
so I'll play my memory tapes of what you used to

50

      say
and I'll hear your voice
your precious voice
when I listen to the Oldies.

Ode to the Moon

by Melia Brokaw

Harken to me, oh lovely Selene,
Night Wanderer, Tidal Guide, Silvered Goddess
With borrowed rays, you glide through heaven,
Over whelming its starry light.
Your beauty bright personifies the feminine,
both mortal and divine,
whether waxing or waning, full orbed or hidden.
Your cycle is the cycle of life.
Teach me to ride your delight of the night,
so that I may avoid the undertow.
Fair lamp of night, all-seeing, vigilant,
Please shine on me with prosperous rays
and to my requests, grant fulfillment.

Can you see the Moon?
by Barbara Ruth

Drunken Words to the Moon

by Callum Hurley

Under this dusky sky, once more we meet,
My Moon, My Lady fairest,
As we have throughout an age now gone
And will, once more, with breath or none

Across the staves of life our story's wrote
My Mother, My firstly love
From one act to next on captious stage
Our bond, inscribed upon this page

Just another sip, casting your shadow
My friend, My companion
To an ernest eye that's all it is
But for we, it's our reason to live

Night Eyes

by Callum Hurley

Upon one eye, thine brother, Helios
The brightness of day that's passed

Upon one eye, thine sister, fair Eos
Luster of a day to come

Selene

by Mab Jones

Sometimes the moon is round; sometimes
she is as slender as a bone. Sometimes she
rolls across the sky, her marble beauty swathed
in silken cloud; at other times her roundness

wanes, her hips are hooks with which she
spears her way. Selene, you teach us not to
hate our form, we women who grow plump,
then thin, then fat; to love our chubby arms,

our skinny limbs, our bodies which are fulsome,
and then not. And so we have our lovers, same
as you: our youthful boys, with curling hair,
smooth backs; their muscles wrapped around us,

lips entwined, and all our dimples lose their
shyness at his hand. Like you, our body's
changeable, fallible, and stark; illuminating
darkness as we follow in your path.

Myths and Stories

Moon in the trees as cars stream by
by Barbara Ruth

Princess Meissa and the Silver Fleece

by Rebecca Buchanan

[Translator's Note: The epic poem *Princess Meissa and the Silver Fleece*[1] by Lycaea of Alexandria[2] disappeared in its entirely sometime around the fourth century of the Common Era. Though it continued to appear in various lists of the great poems of the ancient world — notably Mirzam ibn Fahladin's *Great Works of the Ptolemaic Court*, and Simeon of Constantinople's *Poetical Works Featuring the Hellespont and Surrounding Regions*[3] — the complete poem was lost. Two fragments (sections one and four, below) were known to Saint Winifred of Glastonbury, and are quoted by her in her *Pagan Antecedents of the Blessed Virgin Mary*[4]. A third fragment (the second, below) was discovered by Dr. Sarah Wilkes-Fawkes in 1922, written on four fragments of papyrus which had been used to stuff the chest cavity of an early first century mummy[5]. The fact that another fragment (the third, below) was found as recently as 1991, in a palimpsest languishing in the archives of the Warsaw National Museum of Archaeology and Anthropology[6], offers some hope that there are still fragments out there waiting to be discovered — perhaps even a complete text.[7]]

One (ancient)

  …moaning, ravenous
spirits of the night, loosed
from their prison in the mercury-thick
waters of the marsh of pain.
Naïs, bronze-eyed Queen
of all the Amazons, awoke,
her cry of distress ….[8]

  … Meissa, first
daughter of Naïs, her
twin spears as tongues
of bronze flame ….[9]

Two (1922)

  … white-bearded Pelagius,
eyes burned clean by the God he served;
and Pelagia, his only child,
sworn to the God and beloved by him,
her heart and her body for him alone.[10]

Spears crossed at her back,
hair long and loose,
her feet unshod,
strong-hearted Meissa approached
the mouth of the God ….[11]

  "… ram's wool, gift
of Great Pan to the crystal-hornéd Moon,[12]

which alone may restore the land
of my Mother and my sisters,
bring the dew of the night,
the waters of Selene ...."[13]

Three (1991)

    ... monstrous bull,
hide as brilliant as the full moon,
horns and hooves as sharp
and as black as obsidian.

Eyes burning with the fire of the stars,
the great beast let forth a roar
that ripped the trees from the earth
and the rocks from the mountains.[14]

Spears of flashing bronze in either hand,
Meissa, worthy daughter of Naïs,
called forth her companions,
her sisters bound by blood and oath:

"Come, Laomedia, who shared my cradle
and my first hunt;[15] come, Glycera, whose
blood sings as the sea;[16] come, Euphilia
and Euphrosia, blooded at their mother's
side;[17] come, Pelagia, beloved of the
    Light-Bringer;[18]
come, Ismene, quick of foot and mind;[19]
and you, Gorgophone, true-born daughter of
    Perseus ...."[20]

Four (ancient)

      … came the Lunar Majesty
herself and her glorious retinue:
first, fifty daughters sired by dreaming Endymion,
astride soft-eyed goats and mares
bright as sea foam, and silken ewes,
bare of clothing but for the silver and coral
they wore at ankle and wrist and throat.[21]

Next, Mousaious, called Moon-Fallen,
insomniac son of the slumbering shepherd,
eyes ever open to the wonders and terrors of the
        night.[22]

Arm in arm came Pandeia and Ersa and Nemeia,[23]
their long white hair crowned with wreaths
of asphodel blooms and heliotrope,
lily and laurel,
their footsteps marked with sparkling dew.

And finally the Queen of Midnight herself,
with her curling horns of silver-capped crystal[24]
and hair of deepest sable,
sheer gown tied beneath her full, bare breasts:
called the Luminous One,
called the Rich-Tressed,
called Radiant of Face,
called Mother of Ages:
Selene!

She came astride her favored mount:
a lion, his hide a lustrous abalone,
his mane as darkest night,
whose roar threatened to shake
the stars loose from the firmament.[25]
The ancient earth heaved at the touch
of his massive paws,
the Goddess' laughter echoing between the
        mountains.

Notes

1) The title *Princess Meissa and the Silver Fleece* was widely accepted by classicists and other historians through the nineteenth century. As Dr. Wilkes-Fawkes argues in "Rereadings and Misreadings of Alexandrian Poetry of the Ptolemaic Era" (*Ancient Mediterranean Literary Studies* 4:11, pp 14-28), however, that is based on third- or even fourth-hand incorrect translations of corrupted primary texts. A more accurate translation, but one still not widely accepted, is *Meissa and the Seven Virgins*.

2) Sadly, nothing is known for certain about Lycaea of Alexandria beyond her name; it is not even clear if she was born in Alexandria, although there is evidence that she lived most of her life there. In "Lost Women Poets of Ptolemaic Egypt" (*Feminist Studies in Ancient Literature* 6:12, pp 3-27), Dr. J.J. Dobson makes a strong case for Lycaea having been a lady of the

Ptolemaic court itself, possibly of mixed Greek-Egyptian descent.

3) *Great Works of the Ptolemaic Court* by Mirzam ibn Fahladin (trans. Carl Keane), **Stanley House Publishing**, 1933, pp. 130-131; and *Poetical Works Featuring the Hellespont and Surrounding Regions* by Simeon of Constantinople (trans. S. Efron), **Ace-Bowker Publishers**, 1967, pp. 101.

4) *Pagan Antecedents of the Blessed Virgin Mary* by Saint Winifred of Glastonbury (edited by Miriam Collins), **Schmidt and Sons Publishers**, 1981, pp. 123-128.

5) "The Star in the City of the Sun: Fragments and Other Findings in the Tomb of Stella of Heliopolis" (*Sarcophagus* 4:4, pp. 12-30).

6) The discovery of the palimpsest is worthy of an article all on its own. Suffice to say, the vellum used by the Monks at the Abbey of Saint Theophrastus to create *The Parables of Saint Zlatan* in 1326 CE came from at least four different sources. One of those as-yet unidentified sources contained the fragment of *Princess Meissa and the Silver Fleece* quoted here, which was discovered in 1969 when *The Parables* was placed under a UV light. *The Parables* were then lost in the archives of the Warsaw National Museum of Archaeology and Anthropology, only to be rediscovered again by Amelie Gerard in 1991, a student at the

Sorbonne who was actually looking for a Talmud looted by the Nazis in 1938!

7) This arrangement of the fragments is this translator's best educated guess, i.e., the pieces make sense in relation to one another as they are laid out. See "The Art of (Re)Creation: Poetical Fragments and Figments" by Allison DuBois (*The Leaves of the Tree* 6:3, pp. 29-40) for other suggested arrangements.

8) "Marsh of pain" here refers to the Acheron; while usually a river, several ancient sources describe a marshy area where Charon the Ferryman picks up the souls of the dead and transports them to the Underworld proper. It is unclear whether Lycaea of Alexandria is citing a now-unknown source, or creating something new; either way, it seems that nightmares make their home in the "mercury-thick waters" of the marsh when they are not tormenting mortals. This passage also offers the first hint as to the purpose of Meissa's quest: Queen Naïs is suffering from debilitating nightmares, likely supernatural in origin. Whether the dreams are a punishment or a premonition is unclear.

9) Meissa's first appearance offers several insights into her character. She is not just a warrior, but one particularly skilled in the use of twin spears. The reference to the spears as bronze not only places the story in the mythical/historical past (for both Lycaea of Alexandria and us), but also further re-enforces her identity as daughter of

the "bronze-eyed" Naïs. Additionally, this passage hints that Meissa is not the Queen's only biological daughter, but her eldest; thus, it falls to Meissa to save her mother, her Queen, and her land.

10) Classicists long assumed that the God referred to here is Apollo; this was confirmed by the discovery of the third fragment in 1991 (see notation 18 below). Pelagius is thus at the very least a priest of Apollo, but more probably an oracle. His only child, Pelagia, has followed him into the service of the God, choosing a life of sacred virginity.

11) Meissa here shows due respect for both Apollo and his priest/oracle: she approaches unarmed, with her hair loose (signifying her unmarried, chaste status), and her feet bare (thus identifying herself as a traveler in need of hospitality, one of the most important Greek virtues).

12) Virgil, *Georgics* 3:390 ff — "Twas with gift of such snowy wool, if we may trust the tale, that Pan, Arcadia's god, charmed and beguiled you, O Luna [Selene the Moon], calling you to the depths of the woods; nor did you scorn his call." (translated by Fairclough) It was long assumed by classicists that Virgil here used Pan as a poetic synonym for Endymion, as the latter was a shepherd. However, Wilkes-Fawkes' 1922 discovery casts that assumption into doubt. It seems that there was, indeed, an ancient tradition (which would have been known to

Lycaea of Alexandria's audience, otherwise, why make the reference?) of Pan courting, and winning, at least temporarily, the affection of Selene. He won her favor by presenting her with "ram's wool." This wool was apparently silver in color, not white or off-white, and it possessed extraordinary, magical (even divine) powers (see notation 13, below). Additionally, while this passage adds to the number of ancient sources which describe Selene as having horns — e.g., *Dionysiaca* by Nonnus and *The Fall of Troy* by Quintus Smyrnus — it is the only one of which I am aware which describes them as "crystal."

13) Here is revealed the primary motivation for Meissa's quest: the land of the Amazons is suffering from a severe drought, which threatens mass famine and the end of Amazonian civilization. The Queen's nightmares, referenced in the first passage, may thus be premonitions of this terrible future; alternatively, the nightmares may be a punishment for some wrong perpetrated (by the Queen?), of which the drought is also a part. Only the silver fleece gifted to Selene by Pan can end the drought.

14) It is unclear exactly how this monstrous bull relates to the silver fleece, but the most likely scenario is that the bull is the fleece's guardian. Its obvious lunar qualities led M.L. Nakamura to speculate that the bull might actually be an offspring of Selene herself, or, at the least, a guardian appointed by her (see "A Lunar

Bestiary" in *The Archaeo-Astronomer,* 6:4, p. 46).

15) Based on this passage, it is possible that Laomedia is actually a younger biological sister of Meissa; alternatively, she might be a "sister by oath."

16) Glycera may be a nereid, or the daughter of a nereid, or a daughter of Poseidon. Or, possibly, an ordinary sailor. She may have been responsible for transporting the adventurers to the land of the silver fleece, as Argus did the Argonauts to the Colchis.

17) Likely Amazons, oath-bound to accompany Meissa; and biological sisters (possibly twins, given the similarity of their names).

18) "Light-Bringer" is most commonly a title of Apollo, rather than Helios, thus giving credence to the assumption that Pelagius is a priest/oracle of the former, not the latter.

19) Nothing is known of Ismene outside of this passage.

20) A frustratingly brief appearance by one of the most fascinating women in classical mythology. Gorgophone is one of only two daughters born to Perseus and Andromeda. She is related by blood and/or marriage to Tyndareus, King of Sparta; Helen of Troy, Clytemnestra, Castor and Pollux; Penelope, wife of Odysseus; and Leucippus, father of the Leukippides. In *Princess Meissa and the Silver Fleece,* Lycaea gives Gorgophone her own fantastic adventure,

unconnected to her father, husbands, and children. This passage also places *Meissa* three to four generations before the Trojan War, firmly in the Age of Heroes.

21) Endymion is said to have sired fifty daughters by Selene, while asleep; they are traditionally said to represent the fifty lunar months of the Olympiad.

22) Mousaios is usually understood as Selene's only mortal offspring, a poet and singer of great renown. According to Plato (*Republic* 364d) he is the author of "mystic books." The epithet "Moon-Fallen" comes from Ion of Chios (fragment 30A, *Elegies*). Lycaea of Alexandria here diverges from the known mythology by making the supposedly mortal Mousaios a member of his mother's retinue, and gifted (or cursed) with own unique quality: total insomnia.

23) According to *Homeric Hymn XXXII*, Pandeia is the daughter of Selene by Zeus, as is Ersa (per Alcman, fragment 57). According to the Scholiast on Pindar's *Nemean Ode*, Nemeia is also a daughter of Selene and Zeus. Considering that the first two are closely associated with dew, and nothing is known of the third aside from that single reference, scholars have long assumed that the names all referred to a single Deity. Here, though, Lycaea of Alexandria makes quite clear that she, at least, understands them to be distinct entities; similar in appearance and function, yes, but distinct. It's possible, than,

that Lycaea was either trying to create, or already familiar with, a tradition which treated the Goddesses as a triad (see the three Charites, the three Moirae, and so on).

24) Selene is described in numerous ancient sources as being horned. However, to my knowledge, this is the only text which describes those horns as not only crystal, but as also being decoratively capped in silver. Additionally, referring to them as "curling" strengthens the Goddess' association with the ram, its silver fleece, and, by extension, both Pan and Endymion. R.R. Castillo-Ramirez speculated that Lycaea of Alexandria may have been influenced by depictions of the Egyptian Gods Khnum and Atum ("Egyptian Elements in Hellenistic Poetry: Three Case Studies" [*Ancient Mediterranean Literary Studies* 2:5 pp. 13-14]).

25) This unnamed mount is not the only lion associated with Selene. Aelian (*On Animals* 12:7), Hyginus (*Fabulae* 30), and Seneca (*Hercules Furens* 83ff) all hint that she was somehow responsible for the creation of the Nemean Lion; perhaps even birthed the creature herself. As Selene is usually described as riding a mule, or in a chariot drawn by white horses, it is unclear if the lion mount is Lycaea of Alexandria's invention or if she knew of a tradition which has since been lost — like so much else from the ancient world.

[Author's Note: no such work as *Princess Meissa and the Silver Fleece* exists, or has existed. This piece, while written in honor of the Goddess Selene, is also an homage to those works of the ancient world which truly have been lost — through greed, neglect, apathy, and hate — and which are known now only by their titles or fragmentary quotations in other books. It is a depressingly long list.].

Waiting for Selene

by Terrence P. Ward

"Wait," she says, "for my work is not yet done."

"I must," he rumbles, "but I can scant abide."
"You must," she whispers, as she hurries on her
      way.

So unfolds the fettered tale
of Poseidon, earth-shaker,
and Selene, mistress of the moon.

Mighty son of Kronos though he be,
Poseidon yearned for a woman he could not touch.
Most nights, and some days also, her radiance
would shine upon his glittering realms
rivaling the halls of Olympos where, at times,
he visited, and feasted, and looked upon
her countenance across the table groaning with
      bounty.

Her eyes with his met on occasions not rare,
but always would her face turn from his
as she in turn returned to her duties
to guide the planting and the working
and mark time for all mortals upon the earth
so that they would know that, by its passage,
their own short time of life would too end.

In those fleeting glances, lifetimes may pass
      for a god.
She knew well his desire to know her well,
and never did she spurn the advance

as fair Demeter is said to have done.
Such was her nature, such her work,
that nevertheless she turned away.

"Wait," she says with a look,
"my work is not yet done.
For in me the light of hope must grow
so flowers of the night may bloom in time,
and then turn to darkness, to hide all things
that thrive only in shadows deep
where great Gaea grows her mysteries."

He waits, and in the darkness he yearns
until it grows to melancholy.
Such feelings in a god cannot abide
and so, in the dark of the moon,
he releases his longing through the ground
beneath the temples and homes painstakingly built
by the children of Prometheus.

At times she draws close
boldly, forward, with steady gaze.
At times her approach is circumspect
with eyes downcast, face turned away.
Her moods may shift, and his do join
and yearning rises in his loins
as oceans try to meet the moon above.

If in his mind he truly knows
that to join with him she must,
the obligations given her
turn desire into dust.
Her eyes so often say, "Approach,"

but then she turns away. With sadness
and with sorrow, she adds, "Not today."

In the light of her shining face
to hear himself put off
can sometimes be too much to bear
and be asked his love to doff.
Desire risen, must be spent
and when released, can cause
what seems like divine anger to the likes of mortal
       men.

There may have been another time
when gods were truly free.
A time and place when the universe
required nothing of their divinity.
Perhaps their love developed then
in a world we do not know. Perhaps
the gods knew happiness beyond what we can
       know.

"Wait," she says, "for my work is not yet done."
"I must," he rumbles, "but I can scant abide."
"You must," she whispers, as she hurries on her
       way.

Blue Moon

by Barbara Ruth

The moon came in last night, watched me not sleeping, but I didn't know she was blue until Dolphin told me. She brought it up this morning as explanation for why I'd had a bad night, why she'd had a bad night, why everything has been so weird of late. Dolphin and I had our bad nights separately, but that was only an accident of geography.

Earlier in the evening I went to Claire's house and we'd had another go at the ouija board. She told me about her spirit guides, Goa and Montara. "Spirit guides!" I exclaimed, with the combination of happiness and jealousy I always feel when one of my friends acquires something I want but don't know how to find. "Well, they're also places. Maybe the ouija board wants you to go there. Goa's in West Africa — it's one of the kingdoms of high African culture, like Benin. But Montara is only a few hours away, here in California. We could just up and go, any time." We agreed to make the trip next month.

Finally we got down to it. Claire kept calling, "Goa, Goa, are you there?" Goa answered yes, but she (actually "they" is a more accurate pronoun) didn't want to talk to us.

Instead, the board kept being cryptic, pulling and pushing us here and there with the planchette, and finally reverted to the same boring stuff we'd had before about SJ's VW and TV. TV? Really? I had higher hopes for the astral plane.

One of the things I love about Dolphin is the way she gets so mad when someone does me an injustice. She's a mother bear, that one. I saw on PBS last week that worship of the bear is the oldest known human religion. The circumpolar bear shamans are still going strong, but haven't women always worshipped the moon, long before men recorded things?

And Claire? Just last night, under that old blue moon, she dug me up carrots from her garden to take home with me.

Somehow this all fits together. Last week I saw The Traveling Jewish Theater's performance called "Berlin, Jerusalem, and the Moon." These are likely but problematic — or maybe equally likely to *be* problematic — places to look for one's Jewish identity, according to the play. The best part of that night was discussing it all with Elana. But that happened under a different moon and it's another story.

Moon-Mad

by Rebecca Buchanan

Sweat beaded on Claire's back, collecting along the ridge of her spine to run down into the waistband of her skirt. She shifted on the piano bench, her bottom numb, fingers dancing across the keys. She cast a quick glance up and around the tiny orchestral pit. It was a small space, crammed with four singers, one flutist, one violinist, one harpist, and one percussionist (surrounded by different drums, cymbals, and even a triangle), plus Claire herself and her piano. They were all barely visible in the grey, indirect light of the movie screen and the low, tiny lights clipped to their music stands. Orwell looked like he was about to faint from the heat (again), and Wallis was sneaking a sip from her flask while Lambert bellowed his solo at the top of his lungs; his voice echoed and rebounded from the back of the theater.

Claire skipped her feet across the pedals, and the music accelerated. Dina plucked at her harp, faster and faster, the bun of her hair beginning to unravel, while her daughter DeeDee scrapped a fraying bow across the strings of her violin.

Almost there. Her favorite part.

Behind her, the audience leaned forward in their seats. Colored light filled the theater, the greyish-white giving way to hand-painted cells of brilliant blues, greens, and reds. A collective gasp, followed by oohs and ahhs. Applause and hoorays!

Claire lifted her head, smiling, fingers never missing a key as she watched the climactic scene unfold on the screen above her.

Selene, the hypnotically beautiful Mistress of the Moon, long silver hair streaming behind her as her ox-drawn chariot descended from on high. Her gown was the blue of the sea, and bands of gold graced her throat and arms and wrists. Professor Hecatodorus, tall hat clutched in one hand, pressed his back to the rocket which had carried him to the Goddess' domain. Lunar nymphs swirled around him, arms waving, breasts gleaming. His mouth hung open in astonishment as the chariot dropped onto the lunar surface, the silver hooves of the oxen kicking up clouds of dust.

They tossed their heads, snorting when the Goddess pulled back on the reins, halting the chariot in front of the gaping Professor. The nymphs circled around them, bowing low. Selene smiled down at him benevolently, lips a brilliant red, and spoke.

Wallis almost missed her cue, and once again stumbled over the Professor's name. "My darling Hecatodorus," she intoned, trying for grave and formal, and failing, "welcome to the Moon, my domain, my sanctuary far away from the petty wars and small minds of men."

Orwell took a deep breath, rallying in time to speak his own line. "Beautiful Lady, I humbly thank you."

On the screen high above, the Professor bowed low, sweeping his hat across his body. The Goddess held out her hand, bracelets shimmering, and he stepped into the chariot behind her. With a flick of her wrists, the oxen took off, running faster and faster until they leaped into the heavens, trailing silver dust, growing smaller and smaller while the stars flashed and danced with joy.

The music reached its crescendo, Gregory banging away on the drums while DeeDee sawed at her violin. Claire's fingers skipped and jumped across the keys and then, finally, an echoing silence as The End materialized on the screen.

For a moment, nothing.

And then applause, the audience rising collectively to its feet. There were cheers and whistles and a few people pounded their feet. The house lights came on, gradually brightening.

Claire grinned at the rest of the orchestra, pushing sweaty hair off her forehead. Dina gave her a tired thumbs up. Heaving a sigh of relief, Claire rose and turned to face the audience. As one, the orchestra bowed or curtsied.

The applause grew louder, the whistles and cheers more insistent. Glancing over her shoulder, Claire smiled at the sight of Herr Maihack limping onto the stage from the left, the silver head of his cane winking. The tails of his formal coat waved languidly as he doffed his hat and bowed to the audience. He smiled, as he always did; and, as before, Claire was struck by the underlying note of sadness in that smile.

She could not help but wonder at it. Herr Maihack's film was a phenomenal success, winning over audiences and critics alike across Europe and Canada and the United States, and even Japan. President Roosevelt himself had attended the film's premiere in Washington D.C. Rumor had it that the President had invited Herr Maihack to make a film about Roosevelt's own famous charge up San Juan Hill — and that the German director had politely, but firmly, declined.

The house lights reached their full brightness, and the applause faded. Murmurs and mutterings filled the theater as attendees reached for hats and coats and gloves, and ushers appeared to guide people through the doors and into the lobby and out onto the cold, Chicago streets.

Claire looked up to see that Herr Maihack had already disappeared behind the curtains, stage left. Wiping her hands on her skirt, she began to clean up; she stowed her music sheets inside the piano bench, wiped down the keys and the bench itself, and then rooted around until she found her purse and coat.

Dina hopped over, trying to stomp the numbness out of her legs. She smiled tiredly at Claire. "We're headed over to MacNally's for a nip. Care to join us?"

Claire flicked a look at Wallis, who was staring disconsolately at her empty flask. Dina followed the look.

"Just coffee for that one," she assured Claire.

Claire thought about the tiny empty bed in the tiny empty apartment that was waiting for her, windows taped in a vain attempt to keep out the cold. She pulled on her gloves. "Sure," she finally answered. "Just a couple things to do here, and I'll meet you there."

Dina grinned, wrapped an arm around her daughter, and slipped out of the orchestra pit, around the corner of the stage, and out the back door. Orwell and Wallis and Gregory and the rest followed, murmuring good-nights and good-evenings and see-you-laters. Claire nodded to them all, buttoning up her jacket; she had forgotten her hat again.

The ushers were coming through now, sweeping up the aisles and picking up bits of trash and forgotten pieces of clothing. Nodding, Claire made her way up the aisle and through the lobby. Bright posters announced the films currently playing, and those coming later in the season. The ad for *Palast von das Mond (The Palace of the Moon) Introducing the Glorious Gabriele Espinosa! and Co-Starring Frederick Vanderhoff!* dominated the lobby. Selene, with her bright blue gown and bright red lips, stood regally in the center, an adoring Professor Hecatodorus and scantily-clad lunar nymphs clustered at her feet.

Claire paused, eyes roving over the poster and the beautiful form of the Goddess. Something tugged low in her belly. Longing. A touch of melancholy, and just a bit of anger.

Playing piano at the theater did not pay much — even less then her meager teacher's salary — but she needed it. She needed to be here, in the dark, surrounded by the music, the Goddess lovely and bright overhead. For those few moments, when Professor Hecatodorus flew on his rocket through the stars and found sanctuary on the moon … well, Claire found sanctuary, too. Escape. Freedom from the unwanted attentions of Principal Kline, from the greedy hands and eyes of her landlord, from the cold of her empty bed and her nearly empty pantry.

She sighed, tightening the belt of her coat.

If only ….

Hunching her shoulders, she pushed through the front doors. The marquee overhead flickered and went dark. The sidewalk had emptied rapidly, attendees disappearing in cabs or stumbling down the slippery street to bars and restaurants. Here and there, couples huddled close together, a few trailed by matronly chaperones or protective older brothers. The wind kicked up, swirling snow across the ground and flinging it in her face. Squinting, she looked up to peer through the skyscrapers.

Heavy and swollen, the moon hung in the heavens, a few stars here and there visible against the glare of the city's lights.

The wind whirled up again. Shivering, Claire turned —

— and ran right into Herr Maihack. His cane jabbed her hip.

"Oh! Oh, my goodness. I am so sorry," Claire babbled, reaching out to steady the older man. He frowned at her, seeming to take a few moments to focus on her face and really see her. "Oh, Herr Maihack, my apologies. I didn't see you …."

He smiled gently, lifting a gloved hand to tip his hat. "No need to apologize, fraulein. You were admiring her, *ja*? Like me?" He gestured towards the sky.

"Oh." Claire tilted her head back again, then nodded to him. "Yes, yes I was."

His smile disappeared, his voice taking on a note of yearning as his attention returned to the sky. "She is very beautiful, is she not? Everything a man could desire."

Claire stuffed her hands in her pockets, breath misting. "Yes."

Herr Maihack was silent for a moment, and then he grunted. "Everything a wise man could want."

Claire frowned, confused. "Sir?"

Another long moment of silence. Then, "I see the way you look at her, when she appears, *ja*?

She is mesmerizing. I hunted for a year, trying to find an actress who could embody her — her strength and dignity and ... what is the word? ... charisma." He shook his head regretfully. "I found none. Gabriele ... she is close, but not quite, *ja*? Not truly the Goddess Herself."

Claire swallowed, lips cold. "I don't understand."

Herr Maihack squinted at her, his eyes warm. "I tell you a secret, *fraulein*, because I think you will understand, more than others." He leaned in closer, voice dropping. "It is true."

She blinked. "I ... The film? It's ... true ...?"

His face softened, eyes glazing slightly as his sight turned inward. He looked back to the moon, hat nearly toppling off his balding head "*Ja*. True. There are doors, *fraulein*. Hidden doors to hidden places. That is how I came to Her. Not a rocket ... but I came to Her all the same. And She was *glorious*."

Claire swallowed hard, the cold forgotten.

"I tasted eternity on her lips," he continued. "I could have stayed with her, forever. But I was young and foolish, obsessed with earning the respect of my mortal peers, of winning fame and fortune in the earthly realm. What a damned idiot I was." He shook his head. When he looked back down at her again, she could see the gleam of unshed tears in his eyes. "I tried to go back, when I realized my error. But the door was gone. Every night since, I come out and I call her name, praying that she will forgive a young man's arrogance, and take me home."

Claire opened her mouth, but no words emerged. Her tongue got cold. She closed her mouth with a snap, teeth clacking.

Herr Maihack's expression turned rueful. He tapped the side of his head with his cane. "*Nein*, it is all good up here. I am not mad — at least, not as you are now thinking. Moon-mad, perhaps." He dropped his cane back to the ground, ice cracking beneath its tip. "Very well, then. I am off. I see you tomorrow night, *ja*?"

"I …." Claire hesitated, then nodded. "Yes, I will be here."

Tipping his hat in farewell, he set off down the street and around the corner, coat tails flapping in the wind.

Huddling inside her thin coat, Claire dithered, torn. Sympathy warred with confusion and — deep in her heart — just the tiniest bit of hope.

But no. That was mad. There was no palace on the moon, there were no lunar nymphs, no exalted Goddess with a chariot drawn by snow-hided oxen. That was make-believe, stories told by the ignorant peoples of old, and for the amusement of people today.

It *was* the twentieth century, after all.

Squashing that tiny spark deep in her heart, Claire set off for MacNally's. She had a few cents in her pocket; enough for a sandwich and a warm cup of coffee with a dash of whiskey.

The streetlights flickered overhead and the wind roared suddenly, tearing at her coat and skirt, then died away just as quickly. Weird sounds echoed down the street, bouncing off the corners of the buildings. Blinking against the snow that had been blown into her eyes, Claire stilled, ears perked.

There it was again. Strange scrapes, a clattering. Loud, animal-like woofs. Laughter, sweet with delight.

And then a crack like leather and a clatter of hooves.

And silence.

Claire took a tentative step forward, craning her neck towards the corner of the block. Another hesitant step, biting her lip. And then she was running, slipping and sliding on the ice, grabbing the streetlight as she lost her footing and spun around the corner. She righted herself, knee twisting painfully, and stumbled forward. Off the sidewalk, into the street.

The snow was thin here, but fresh, and the tracks were clear. They began in the middle of the road, appearing out of nowhere, and then disappeared back into nothingness.

Oxen hooves and the wheels of a chariot.

An abandoned cane with a silver head lay near the left-hand track.

Snow crunching beneath her shoes, Claire made her slow way over to it. Fingers numb, she bent to pick it up; it was heavy. Just as slowly, she straightened, gaze sliding from the cane, to the tracks, and up to the wide moon and sharp stars.

There are doors, he had said, and she laughed.

[Author's Note: The Library of Congress estimates that 70% of American silent films have been completely lost. *Le Voyage dans la Lune*, created by and staring Georges Méliès, is one of the few European films to survive. An international success on its initial release in 1902, it was extensively pirated by other studios. Its length (eighteen minutes, unusual for the time), its high production values, innovative special effects, and quality storytelling were extremely influential. The scene in which the rocket lands in the Moon's eye remains one of the most memorable and recognizable images in all of cinema.]

The Fairytale

by Melia Brokaw

Hey Didal, Didal
Mew with your fiddle
Of the cow thrown over the Moon
Whose dogs howled
To see her fouled
Since Discia ran away from Typhoon!"

shouted the child as she ran into the workshop.

"Ha, Ha. Aren't you a bit old for stories? And don't call me Didal," muttered Daedalus as he bent over his workbench.

"But I like your stories. Especially this one and you haven't told it in a while," pleaded the girl.

"Why should I, little one? You know it by heart. Besides, didn't I just hear Cleitus sing it last night?"

"Please?! It is so much better when you tell it. He does not tell it half so well as you!"

"Well I suppose, but you will have to listen without my 'fiddle' as I must work while I talk." He glanced up from his project in time to see the child reach up to grab something that caught her eye on the table. "Touch that and there will be no tale."

The child quickly put her hands behind her back and stepped away from the table, away from temptation, eager to hear her favorite tale.

"Now how does it go?" he muttered, dropping a tool at his feet.

The child quickly ran over and picked it up, prompting him with "Typhoon, a giant born of his mother's anger ...."

"Ah yes. Thank you." Taking the tool from her, he said, "Are you sure you don't want to tell me the tale?"

"No, No. Please, Daedalus, please?!"

"Ok, Ok. Typhoon a giant born of his mother's anger ...."

"Because Zeus bore Athene ...," pipes up the young voice.

"Who is telling this tale again?"

"Sorry. I'll be quiet," said the girl as she sat at his feet.

Typhoon, a giant born
of his mother's anger
of his mother's revenge
for the daughter begot
by her husband alone.
Typhoon was fair of face
but of such bad temper
that he appeared monstrous
to all on the heavenly plane.
So gifted, he was, to Echidna
Mother of all Monsters
to raise as she saw fit
which is to say
his upbringing did nothing

to improve upon his temper.
In a nearby village
there was a maiden
lovely of form and face
called Discia, daughter
of a discus maker.
Typhoon was in love
with the gentle maiden
who found him terrifying.
One festival evening,
Typhoon made his way
with flowers and gifts
to woo the timid girl.
By Selene's lamp,
he found her in a glade
not alone, but with another
a lover, unknown.
Roaring with anger,
Typhoon rampages
set to kill his rival
only to trip upon
a moon-shadowed root
hitting his head
consciousness fled
allowing for escape.
The lovers gone,
never to be seen again.
Typhoon mourned
the loss of his love
and bore a grudge
blaming bright Selene

for the loss of his hopes.
The next time he saw Mene
he was wiping the sweat
from his fevered brow
as he cussed and guided
the oxen pulled plow.
He glancing upwards
to see a silvered chariot
gliding across the heavens.
Its horned charioteer
beautiful to behold.
Anger in his giant's heart
fueled his enormous strength.
Bellowing Typhoon grabbed
the ox from the plough tree
threw it at his offender.
The cow flew so high
it sailed over the moon
startling her in her course
causing hounds to bay
in confusion and distress.
From this day forward
until subdued by Zeus
many a bovine was lost
as Typhoon tried to knock
Selene out of the sky.

Daedalus finished his task as his story
ended. He looked up in time to see the girl
galloping out the door. Just as she left his sight, he
heard a clanging noise. One of the servants

muttered darkly as the child yelled, "You missed Typhoon! Again!"

[Editor's Note: the monstrous son of Hera alone (or Gaea and Tartarus in other tales), is also variously known as Typhon, Typhoeus, Typhaon, and Typhos.]

The Man in the Moon

by Melia Brokaw

The man in the moon? Eh, there is no man in the moon but there is the image of one upon it…

Sit down, sit down. Grandma Cece will tell you ….

There once was a prince who fled his home … the sun had not quite left the heavens.

Why? Some heartache or embarrassment or some such thing I would imagine … now hush. Where was I? Oh yes. He fled into the coming night and was set upon by thieves. The only one to see his dire predicament was Mene. He —

What? What do they teach you in school?! Mene! The moon!

The prince called out to Mene, "Oh bright one aid me and I will do you much honor!" His opponents became moonstruck for long enough that he was able to overcome them and escape. Now this prince had always had an interest in the skies, an amateur astronomer you might say. So to honor Mene, he vowed to stay with her until she returned to that exact place in the sky that she was when she aided him.

At first he thought this would mean just 28 days, which was perfect as it allowed him to avoid home for all that time. Yet when that time period was up, he realized that the moon was not at the same place in the sky that she was when he started his observations. He could not leave the fields until she reached that spot again or be forsworn. So he moved into an old hut and lived like a common sheep herder. When Mene was found in the sky, the prince was there looking up at her. Often he would be found in a field asleep, bathed in the bright rays of Mene. When she was not to be seen, he was going about the princely business of livin'.

In this manner, the prince spent fifty lunar cycles staring up at Mene in fulfillment of his vow. At its completion, he erected a pillar dedicated to Selene, the bright one who defended him at a time when he needed it most. Upon becoming king, he even commemorated this vow with games every fifty lunar months. Later, he chose as his successor which ever son that won in these games. Some say that this is the actually start of the Olympics. Zeus was a late comer to those ….

Eh? What? How does this relate to the man on the moon? Haven't you figured it out? The prince was Endymion. His piety was so admired by Mene, who he called Selene, that she had the image of his face seared on to that floating rock in his memory. The once clear features have been worn down over time, of course but —

That isn't what your teachers say? Well then why are you asking me? Don't you think I've got better things to do then waste your time?! Kids these days … get on with you!

Lunacy

by Jackie Davis Martin

The girl — Selena — walked down the hill in the cold, under a moon bright and full in the dark winter sky. It was a long time ago, maybe the fifties. She carried a small case, like a train case, filled with dancing shoes — tap shoes and ballet shoes and even toe shoes, although those caused her a great deal of pain since she was chunky. Chubby. She was twelve years old and knew the fullness of her body, now wrapped in a wool stadium jacket, and long plaid shawl, long enough so that the ends trailed down the back of the jacket. It was the style. She liked going to dancing school two evenings a week, liked the independence, even, of taking the streetcar then the bus back home, a route she was on now in the dark cold, under the clear moon.

As she walked down the hill, she wrapped the shawl around a second time, keeping her neck warm. She wore ankle socks and loafers with pennies in them for luck. Her glasses felt like ice cubes on her cheeks, cheeks that betrayed her with their eruptions. Her mother was going to take her to another doctor to see what could be done.

The loafers made a click-click sound on the sidewalk, the bare branches of trees overhead broke the moon into puzzle pieces that rearranged themselves at the end of the block. Her breath puffed in front of her and, under a streetlight, she deliberately made O's, pretending to smoke. Her father — all the men in her family — smoked. None of the women did.

Tonight her dancing teacher, Diedre, had asked her, privately, if she had fallen off the roof. The question came after Selena had completed a ballet combination with an awkward little jump. Selena had clutched her stomach, which hurt a bit, and stepped back to the barre to watch the others. She always was called on first because she remembered everything, the others watching. The girls — eight in number, when they all showed up, like tonight — had been in the same class since they were six. Selena had frowned at the question, picturing the roofs outside on the big Victorians. "Your monthly," Diedre whispered. "Do you have your visitor?" Selena reddened and admitted, yes. She wondered if Diedre — and the others — had noticed the extra bulk in her leotard. She was twelve and embarrassed.

The hill from dancing school led down to the main street of the small town, a part where there were a line of drab row homes, two boarded-up stores, and a vacant lot of frozen grass that looked like a tundra. She had just learned that word in social studies and liked it. The world looked like a tundra. These blocks would open into more lively ones, a shoe store, a cigar store, the bar where her dad worked for her uncle. Her hands were frozen in the mittens. Maybe the cold, the moon, would clear her skin.

A car was moving slowly along the street and it took a few minutes before Selena realized the car was following her. It was a big car; even in the moonlight she could see that it was rusty in spots, and two men were in the front seat. One was driving and the other was rolling down his window. "Hey!" he called, smiling. "Want a ride, sweetheart?"

Selena looked around. She was alone — they meant her. The car rode along at the pace she was walking, next to her. She was bundled up, lumpy and unattractive; they were after her.

She shook her head and walked faster, head down. The car moved with her, silent under the moon. She would be in the livelier area soon — she had to keep walking. "Hey!" the voice cried again. "Sweetheart! Why don't you come over here, huh?"

The car inched to the curb, to the edge of the sidewalk. The door opened; Selena could see a man placing his foot on the street, holding the door. She ran. Her shawl fell and her case bumped against her bare legs and she ran, the loafers hard and heavy against the sidewalk, ran three desperate blocks until she hurled herself through the doors of Lou's Lounge. The room was heavy with beer and smoke but her dad, in his bow tie, was behind the bar. "Daddy!" she cried. They all turned.

He drove her home — leaving the other bartender to fend for an hour. His terror seemed greater than her own. "There are lunatics out there!" he muttered. "Why does your mother let you — oh,

Christ, I let you, too! You seem so capable. But it's lunacy. We'll have to make other arrangements."

The car was warm and comforting, like her Dad, and she listened to him and to the soft whir of the heater, her heart still beating thickly from the encounter, the run. A man had called her Sweetheart.

Rituals and Prose Writings

Full Moon with Vivid Aurora
by Callum Hurley

Rite for Selene

by Callum Hurley

This is a general rite, to which I attach a particular mention to Selene on most days, but always on days significant to the lunar cycle (the new, full and quarter moons specifically). As I am also a practicing Zen Buddhist I usually, but not always, perform this after meditation. As the purpose of meditation to a Buddhist is to the benefit and salvation of all sentient beings (mortal and otherwise), this is a fitting time for my to do so;

My Lords and Ladies of Olympus,
Netjer of the Glistening East,
Great Lords of the North,
Glorious Kami, spirits and Devas
Fair Akua of the Southern Ocean
Revered Bodhissatvas and venerable Tathagata
And all aspects of the One, in every form

I pray:

I humbly implore that you will accept this, my
        devotion
And that our lives may be bound by order, and
        Ma'at
And good works, to your glory, that may stake alive
        within the hearts of men;
Chaos that gnaws at our form may ever be held at

bay,
That we may to age abundant be spared, and when
      time should come —
For our to step at Hermes road unto your wait —
That we may without remorse, or regret.
Above all, Lords of all, may your presence may be
      felt in my heart
If ever I have pleased you, true to the spirit of
      reciprocity,
and the principle of Nepthelmaus
And may we be as one;
free from suffering, as happy and as healthy as fates
      decree,
we together, at peace.

(A moment's silence, then continue)

My Lady Selene, Maiden of my heart and mind
and my dearest Guardian star
I thank you always for your friendship,
Your kindness, your patience, your guidance,
Above all others, may you be in my heart always
Your Lunessence to light my way, your shadow to
      state my faith
Forever, as we.

(Other particular devotionals are often here
attached and can be of any number or kind. I always
attach the four Bodhissatva vows of Mahayana
Buddhism, but have omitted them here. Often
requests or offerings are presented here. Hermes,

Persephone, Athena, and Bast are common Deity choices.)

The Gift of Selene

by Jenny Elliot

I learned about Selene while working with Moon Goddesses. The first image I came upon was a depiction of her riding her chariot, flanked by winged-horses. It was so warm and comforting that I often use it as the background of my computer as well as meditating on the image itself. I am a complete night-owl and moon gazing is the best way to settle my emotions and work on grounding my energy. I was searching for a deeper connection and found it through her stone, Selenite. Viewing the stone online, I thought of how peaceful it appeared.

I usually go to bed as the sun rises, and I have a hard time falling asleep. I have used stones, specially-made sleep pillows as well as items from other Priestesses that are made for helping one sleep peacefully. My windows are covered by dark purple curtains to keep the light out. I learned that Selene is called upon for sleep. This intrigued me, since I have had insomnia and nightmares since childhood. My fellow Priestess gifted me with a Selenite wand last year and it has become one of my great treasures.

The first time I held it, I felt such comfort and love. Knowing how Selene struggled with love, I felt her loving presence course through the stone. She is a Titan, and is not mentioned often in pagan discussions. I could feel her sadness at being set aside for more popular Deities. I went home and held the wand in both hands. I was overcome by beautiful images of the universe and the feeling of floating on clouds.

I recently bought a Selenite ring and I wear it to bed each night. Since then I have fallen asleep faster, have fewer nightmares, and can remember my dreams. Before my dreams often told the same story; re-running through the past and reliving the bad memories. Now my dreams are helping me move forward and hold clues to what actions I should take. It is incredible to have this transition happen after so many years.

I am so thankful to have Selene in my life. She reminds me to look ahead, let the past go, and surrender to the wisdom of my dreams. The deities live for love as we do, and as we honor them, they bring us love that never dies. I hope more people discover her precious stone and use it with love and devotion.

Drinking Alone Beneath the Moon

by Callum Hurley

The full Moon is a very special time for me, and it is something that I ensure to observe every month, regardless of what else may be happening in my life. I find this to be my anchoring point to the world, my binding to the cycles and immediate realities of the human experience. I have not always been able to perform the full rites and rituals or delver my daily prayer for example but I have always acknowledged this occasion.

On the Morning
Greet the full moon with my awakening breath, with the phrase; "My dearest lady, my Selene fair. Today my faith is vowed once more, be at peace"/

In the Evening
Once the evening arrives and the Moon is visible I pour myself some manner of drink (sometimes alcoholic, sometimes not), excuse myself from company and go alone to enjoy it beneath her, sharing a libation with Selene in the process. I make a point to avoid formality and ritual at this point, speaking instead with the moon as to an old friend. This feels right to me, I have revered the Moon for as long as I can remember and it feels like a relationship that precludes conscious thought or establishment.

This particular ritual is inspired by my lifelong favourite poem: 'Drinking alone beneath the Moon' by the Chinese poet Li Bai. Once the glasses are empty I always bow and leave with a fragment of the verse, my favourite, which is inscribed upon the bespoke made bronze coin of Selene that I always carry:

"My Lady, our bond will outshine all Earthly love
Next time we'll meet beyond the stars above."

Selene and Endymion
by Stefano Torelli

Appendix A: Ancient Hymns

Homeric Hymn (32) to Selene [from *The Homeric Hymns and Homerica with an English Translation* by Hugh G. Evelyn-White. Homeric Hymns. Cambridge, MA., *Harvard University Press*; London, William Heinemann Ltd. 1914.]

And next, sweet voiced Muses, daughters of Zeus, well-skilled in song, tell of the long-winged[1] Moon. From her immortal head a radiance is shown from heaven and embraces earth; and great is the beauty that from her shining light. The air, unlit before, glows with the light of her golden crown, and her rays beam clear, whensoever bright Selene having bathed her lovely body in the waters of Ocean, and donned her far-gleaming raiment, and yoked her strong-necked, shining team, drives on her long-maned horses at full speed, at eventime in the mid-month: then her great orbit is full and then her beams shine brightest as she increases. So she is a sure token and a sign to mortal men.

Once the Son of Cronos was joined with her in love; and she conceived and bare a daughter Pandia, exceeding lovely amongst the deathless gods.

Hail, white-armed goddess, bright Selene, mild, bright-tressed queen! And now I will leave you and sing the glories of men half-divine, whose deeds minstrels, the servants of the Muses, celebrate with lovely lips.

***

Orphic Hymn (8) to Selene [from *The Hymns of Orpheus*. Translated by Taylor, Thomas (1792). *University of Pennsylvania Press*, 1999. (current edition)]

Hear, Goddess queen, diffusing silver light, bull-horn'd and wand'ring thro' the gloom of Night.
With stars surrounded, and with circuit wide Night's torch extending, thro' the heav'ns you ride:
Female and Male with borrow'd rays you shine, and now full-orb'd, now tending to decline.
Mother of ages, fruit-producing Moon [Mene], whose amber orb makes Night's reflected noon:
Lover of horses, splendid, queen of Night, all-seeing pow'r bedeck'd with starry light.
Lover of vigilance, the foe of strife, in peace rejoicing, and a prudent life:
Fair lamp of Night, its ornament and friend, who giv'st to Nature's works their destin'd end.
Queen of the stars, all-wife Diana hail! Deck'd with a graceful robe and shining veil;
Come, blessed Goddess, prudent, starry, bright, come moony-lamp with chaste and splendid light,

Shine on these sacred rites with prosp'rous rays, and pleas'd accept thy suppliant's mystic praise.

***

Fragment by Sappho [from *Stung with Love: Poems and Fragments of Sappho.* Translated by Aaron Poochigian (2009). Penguin Classics collection 2009 (Current Edition)]

"The Astera hide away their shining form around lovely Selene, when in all her fullnesss she shines over all the earth."

Appendix B: Epithets and Other Ancient Aspects of Selene

A number of ancient Hellenic Goddesses were associated with the Moon, but it was only Selene who was represented as the Moon itself incarnate. Other figures such as Artemis and Hecate also developed strong Lunar associations, and were often depicted thusly in Renaissance art, to the confusion of many.

Selene was regarded by ancient authors as a Titaness, a member of the older pantheon of Gods succeeded (i.e. overthrown) by the Olympians, but had remained on good terms and retained her post, often said to be due to her aid fighting against the Titan monster Typhon. This reputation as a 'benign Titaness' gave her strong links with reconciliation and peace.

She is usually depicted as a beautiful woman commanding a chariot drawn by a pair of winged steeds, either Oxen (to which the 'horns' of the full Moon are likened) or silver horses.

Selene was not at the center of many myths, the most prominent being her great love of the shepherd prince Endymion, who was granted immortality by Zeus and set to slumber in a cave to which Selene would visit by night. Another myth, regarding her seduction by the nature-God Pan, symbolised her strong link with nature and the cycles of the World.

Owing to the Lunar method of measuring the year, she was also celebrated as the Goddess of the month (often under the name 'Mene') and had a strong connection with the passing of time. She was also celebrated as the 'Mother of Dew', which was believed to have a healthy nourishing effect upon the plants and animals of the World.

She was regarded as the Sister/Half-Sister of Helios and also of Eos (the dawn), having all been sired by Hyperion (a Titan God of Light) and another variable Goddess. She was also variously attributed as the Mother of Pandeia, Ersa, Nemeia, The Horai, The Menai, The Nemean Lion, Mousaios, and Narcissus.

Epithets

Μηνη – Mênê – 'Month'

Αιγλη – Aiglê – 'Gleaming/Radiant'

Πασιφαε – Pasiphae – 'All-Shining'

Ειλειθυια – Eileithyia – 'Reliever'

Cult Centers

Selene was perceived by the ancients as something of a universal figure on account of her very visible and prominent place in the night sky, and thus it was not considered 'as necessary' to create Sacred Places for her worship. Accordingly temples and cult centers of Selene were relatively uncommon, though this in no way reflects the level of esteem afforded to the Goddess.

Nevertheless, Selene was still prominent in some areas of the Hellenic World

I) Thalamai in Lakedaimonia.
Here a spring sacred to both Selene and Helios (The Sun) was said to flow and be drunk from by adherents.

II) Ellis in Southern Greece.

III) The Aventine Hill in Rome.
Here Selene (in her Roman aspect 'Luna') was worshipped at the end of each Lunar Month

IV) Other temples in general; such as the Parthenon.
As a celestial figure, Selene commonly appears in general temple decoration, for example her image can still be seen today upon the Parthenon's East pediment.

Sources:

Hesiod, *Theogeny*, Greek epic C8th-7th B.C.
Pausanias, *Description of Greece* 3. 26. 1 (trans. Jones)
Pausanias, *Description of Greece* 6. 24. 6
Homeric Hymn 32 to Selene (trans. Evelyn-White) (Greek epic C7th - 4th B.C.)
Ovid, *Metamorphoses* 7. 179 ff (trans. Melville) (Roman epic C1st B.C. to C1st A.D.)
Ovid, *Fasti* 3. 883 ff (trans.Boyle) (Roman poetry C1st B.C. to C1st A.D.)

Appendix C: Our Contributors

Melia Brokaw is a devotee of Zeus and Isis who lives high in the Colorado Rocky Mountains. She loves her job at the local library. When she isn't chasing her 8 year old, she can be found reading, writing or stitching. She is the editor of *From Cave to Sky: A Devotional Anthology in Honor of Zeus* previously published by *Bibliotheca Alexandrina*. Her author blog is OakenScrolls.wordpress.com.

Rebecca Buchanan is the editor of the literary Pagan magazine, *Eternal Haunted Summer*, and the editor-in-chief of *Bibliotheca Alexandrina*. She has been previously published in *Bards and Sages Quarterly*, *Gingerbread House*, *Luna Station Quarterly*, *Nebula Rift*, and *New Realm*, among other venues. Her first short story collection, *A Witch Among Wolves, and Other Pagan Tales*, was just released by *Asphodel Press*.

Vonnie Winslow Crist, MS Professional Writing, is a Pushcart Nominee, the winner of a Maryland State Arts Council Poetry Award (USA), and the author of two award-winning collections of poetry: *Essential Fables* and *River of Stars*. Her poems have appeared in publications in Finland, Italy, Canada, Australia, the UK, and the USA.

Jenny Elliott is a Strega by blood and a Licensed Priestess of Hekate in the Fellowship of Isis. She is known as "Hekate's Lady" and has contributed to *Circle Magazine* as well as *Daughter of the Sun: A Devotional Anthology in Honor of Sekhmet*. She spends time creating art, singing, writing, reading, performing rituals, and spending time with her loved ones or in nature. Contact her at Hekateslady@facebook.com

Karen Greenbaum-Maya, retired clinical psychologist, German major, two-time Pushcart nominee, and occasional photographer, no longer lives for Art, but still thinks about it a lot. Her photos and poems appear in journals and anthologies with remarkable frequency. Her first full sentence was, "Look at the moon!" She looks for the new moon and the old moon because they show her that, fundamentally, the universe is unrolling as it must. She co-hosts Fourth Sundays, a poetry series in Claremont, California. She has published two chapbooks through *Kattywompus Press*: *Burrowing Song*, a collection of prose poems, and *Eggs Satori*. For links go to: http://www.cloudslikemountains.blogspot.com/.

Callum Hurley is the editor of this anthology. He has had an abiding and lifelong love of poetry and mythology in general, and that relating to the Moon in particular, which he has loved and revered for as long as he can recall. He would best describe himself as an eclectic polytheist, who draws philosophically upon many different cultures and traditions and is very passionate about traveling widely in better pursuit of that aim. He can be reached at callumhurley@hotmail.com

Mab Jones is a "unique talent" (*The Times*) who has read her poems all over the UK, in the US, Ireland, France, and Japan. She runs the literary e-magazine *Black Sheep Journal* and is a freelance writer for the *New York Times*. www.mabjones.com

Gerri Leen lives in Northern Virginia and originally hails from Seattle. She has stories and poems published or accepted in: *Daily Science Fiction*, *Escape Pod*, *Grimdark*, *Sword and Sorceress XXIII*, *She Nailed a Stake Through His Head: Tales of Biblical Terror,* and others. She edited *A Quiet Shelter There,* which benefits homeless animals (*Hadley Rille Books*). See more at http://www.gerrileen.com.

Jackie Davis Martin's most recent stories have appeared in *Flash, Flashquare, Enhance, Fractured West, Bluestem,* and *Thrice Fiction,* and are included in several current anthologies: *Modern Stories* (ed. Michelle Richmond), *Love on the Road* (ed. Sam Tranum), *Life is a Rollercoaster* (ed. A.J.Huffman) and *Out Past Loves* (*Spruce Mountain*). A story recently placed first in the *New Millennium Writings* contest, and another story second place in *On the Premises*. A memoir,

Surviving Susan, was published in 2012. She teaches at City College of San Francisco.

With his first collection of poetry, *Manhattan Plaza*, **James B. Nicola** follows poets Frank O'Hara and Stanley Kunitz and humorist Robert Benchley as a New York author originally from Worcester, Massachusetts. His second collection, *Stage to Page: Poems from the Theater*, will be out in 2016. He has been widely published in periodicals including the *Southwest*, *Atlanta*, *Lullwater* and *Texas Reviews*, *Tar River*, *Lyric*, *Nimrod*, *Blue Unicorn*, and two previous anthologies from *Bibliotheca Alexandrina*. James won the Dana Literary Award, a People's Choice award (from *Storyteller*), a *Willow Review* award, one Rhysling and two Pushcart nominations, and was featured poet at *New Formalist*. A Yale grad and stage director by profession, his nonfiction book *Playing the Audience* won a *Choice* award. Also a composer, lyricist, and playwright, his children's musical *Chimes: A Christmas Vaudeville* premiered in Fairbanks, Alaska, with Santa Claus in attendance on opening night. Visit sites.google.com/site/jamesbnicola.

K.S. Roy (also known as Khryseis Astra) is an artist, astrologer, and writer living in Western Pennsylvania. She is particularly devoted to Hekate, Hermes, Persephone, Apollon, and the Muses. She has been the Graphic Designer for *He Epistole*, a

Hellenic Polytheist newsletter issued by Neokoroi, the editor for *Guardian of the Road: A Devotional Anthology in Honor of Hermes,* and is currently at work on a devotional art series for the Theoi.

Barbara Ruth writes at the intersection of Potowatomi and Ashkenazi, disabled and neuroqueer, fat and yogi, not this and not that. She has memoirs, poetry, and fiction appearing in the following anthologies, published in 2015 and 2016: *Tales of Our Lives: Women and Health*; *Biting the Bullet: Essays on Women and Courage; QDA: Queer Disability Anthology;* and *Les Cabinets des Polythéistes* and *Garland Of the Goddess* from *Bibliotheca Alexandrina.*

Kyria Skotas is a writer, poet, and artist currently living in California with her partner and cat. A walker of many roads and an unapologetic witch, she practices the use of words and art as functions of power, both personal and divine. She is an animist, seer, and polytheist devoted to many, with a host of beasts, monsters, and spirits to keep her busy.

Her writings have been published in *Queen of Olympos: A Devotional Anthology for Hera and Iuno* (*Bibliotheca Alexandrina,* 2013) and *Crossing the River: An Anthology of Sacred Journeys* (Bibliotheca Alexandrina, 2014).

Kyria was among the founding parties of *Crowned by Star and Sky*, a quarterly devotional zine in honor of the Queen of Heaven. She has worked as an editor and sometime contributor of the zine from (its founding in) the fall of 2014 through the winter of 2015.

You can find Kyria in many places online, and keep up with her and her work via her new blog: shadowinscriber.wordpress.com

Luque Spinner is a polytheist devoted to her Ancestor Gods. She is a wanderer at heart, currently going to school in the Southwest but growing up south of the Mason-Dixon, and likes pulling artistic influences into her writing.

Madaline Stevens is a young author who hopes to make a difference with her writing.

Terence P. Ward realized he was Pagan after he bought his own copy of *Drawing Down the Moon* in 1988. His religious practices since have included being bound to a Wiccan coven, walking sacred trails as a backpacking Pagan or Gaiaped, raising energy with a number of loosely-organized collections of people, and being tapped by the Olympian gods. He is a polytheist with pantheistic and monistic sympathies, an animist approach to the world, and a respect for his ancestors. His personal practice includes daily offerings to Poseidon and weekly meeting for worship with his fellow Quakers.

Matthew Wilson has had over 150 appearances in such places as *Horror Zine*, *Star*Line*, *Spellbound*, *Alban Lake*, *Apokrupha Press*, *Space & Time Magazine*, and many more. He is currently editing his first novel and can be contacted on twitter @matthew94544267

Appendix D: About Bibliotheca Alexandrina

Ptolemy Soter, the first Makedonian ruler of Egypt, established the library at Alexandria to collect all of the world's learning in a single place. His scholars compiled definitive editions of the Classics, translated important foreign texts into Greek, and made monumental strides in science, mathematics, philosophy and literature. By some accounts over a million scrolls were housed in the famed library, and though it has long since perished due to the ravages of war, fire, and human ignorance, the image of this great institution has remained as a powerful inspiration down through the centuries.

To help promote the revival of traditional polytheistic religions we have launched a series of books dedicated to the ancient gods of Greece and Egypt. The library is a collaborative effort drawing on the combined resources of the different elements within the modern Hellenic and Kemetic communities, in the hope that we can come together to praise our gods and share our diverse understandings, experiences and approaches to the divine.

A list of our current and forthcoming titles can be found on the following page. For more information on the Bibliotheca, our submission requirements for upcoming devotionals, or to learn about our organization, please visit us at neosalexandria.org.

Sincerely,

The Editorial Board
of the Library of Neos Alexandria

Current Titles

Written in Wine: A Devotional Anthology for
      Dionysos
Dancing God: Poetry of Myths and Magicks
Goat Foot God
Longing for Wisdom: The Message of the Maxims
The Phillupic Hymns
Unbound: A Devotional Anthology for Artemis
Waters of Life: A Devotional Anthology for Isis and
      Serapis
Bearing Torches: A Devotional Anthology for
      Hekate
Queen of the Great Below: An Anthology in Honor
      of Ereshkigal
From Cave to Sky: A Devotional Anthology in
      Honor of Zeus
Out of Arcadia: A Devotional Anthology for Pan
Anointed: A Devotional Anthology for the Deities
      of the Near and Middle East
The Scribing Ibis: An Anthology of Pagan Fiction in
      Honor of Thoth
Queen of the Sacred Way: A Devotional Anthology
      in Honor of Persephone

Unto Herself: A Devotional Anthology for
    Independent Goddesses
The Shining Cities: An Anthology of Pagan Science
    Fiction
Guardian of the Road: A Devotional Anthology in
    Honor of Hermes
Harnessing Fire: A Devotional Anthology in Honor
    of Hephaestus
Beyond the Pillars: An Anthology of Pagan Fantasy
Queen of Olympos: A Devotional Anthology for
    Hera and Iuno
A Mantle of Stars: A Devotional Anthology in
    Honor of the Queen of Heaven
Crossing the River: An Anthology in Honor of
    Sacred Journeys
Ferryman of Souls: A Devotional for Charon
By Blood, Bone, and Blade: A Tribute to the
    Morrigan
Potnia: An Anthology in Honor of Demeter
The Queen of the Sky Who Rules Over All the
    Gods: A Devotional Anthology in Honor of
    Bast
From the Roaring Deep: A Devotional for Poseidon
    and the Spirits of the Sea
Daughter of the Sun: A Devotional Anthology in
    Honor of Sekhmet
Seasons of Grace: A Devotional in Honor of the
    Muses, the Charites, and the Horae
Lunessence: A Devotional for Selene

Forthcoming Titles

Garland of the Goddess: Tales and Poems of the Feminine Divine

Les Cabinets des Polythéistes: An Anthology of Pagan Fairy Tales, Fables, and Nursery Rhymes

The Dark Ones: Tales and Poems of the Shadow Gods

First and Last: A Devotional for Hestia

Dauntless: A Devotional for Ares and Mars

At the Gates of Dawn and Dusk: A Devotional for Eos and Aurora

Shield of Wisdom: A Devotional Anthology in Honor of Athena

Megaloi Theoi: A Devotional Anthology for the Dioskouroi and Their Families

Sirius Rising: A Devotional Anthology for Cynocephalic Deities

Printed in France by Amazon
Brétigny-sur-Orge, FR

19505430R00071